Letters
to
Africans

Letters
to
Africans

Leon Tuam

authorHOUSE®

AuthorHouse™
1663 Liberty Drive
Bloomington, IN 47403
www.authorhouse.com
Phone: 1-800-839-8640

Published by AuthorHouse   06/15/2012

ISBN: 978-1-4772-1694-1 (sc)
ISBN: 978-1-4772-1695-8 (e)

Library of Congress Control Number: 2012910331

Any people depicted in stock imagery provided by Thinkstock are models, and such images are being used for illustrative purposes only.
Certain stock imagery © Thinkstock.

This book is printed on acid-free paper.

Because of the dynamic nature of the Internet, any web addresses or links contained in this book may have changed since publication and may no longer be valid. The views expressed in this work are solely those of the author and do not necessarily reflect the views of the publisher, and the publisher hereby disclaims any responsibility for them.

DEDICACE

For the humiliated people of dignity of Africa.

Contents

Native nest

I lived on my native Nest and strongly
I believed in the benefits of goodness,
I believed in the benefits of peaceful words.

I tearfully left my native Nest,
Crossed the Atlantic Ocean and strongly
I believed in the benefits of goodness,
I believed in the benefits of peaceful words.

But when I turned back and saw heavy guns
Silence the lives of thousands of mouths,
When I saw bombs and created poverty,
Hunger and diseases silence children,
Silence adults,
Silence elders,
Silence our villages, streets and cities,

I met on my way some words
That I never dreamed of.
I looked at them and they smiled at me.
They talked to me,
They told me that they were the true friends,
I hesitated to pay attention to them,
They touched me and showed seriousness,
They told me that from that time
They were my best friends;

I found them helpful,
I found them precious.
Compared to the bombs,
Compared to the created diseases,
Those words were nothing.

I bent,
I collected and
I started using them profusely,
To stone the night, to stone and
Stone the night, the African night.

African Golgothas

Africans,
We have walked many paths of suffering,
We have walked many roads of contempt,
We have walked many boulevards of divisions,
We have walked many streets of destabilizations,
Walked many highways of humiliations,
Walked those of frustrations and discriminations,
And walked those of wrong negotiations and peace,
Wondering when we will see their ends;

Sufferings spring out of our faces
Like an army of worms from dry carrions
Which are tickled by a heavy rain.
Golgotha, Golgotha, African Golgotha!

Golgotha, we climb you,
And once at your peak,
Another Golgotha calmly awaits us;
We climb it and at its peak,
We hear a strong call and as we look,
We discover another Golgotha
That is taller and bigger than the previous ones.
Golgotha, Golgotha, African Golgotha!

Black nights, deep African long nights!
Everlasting deep nights!
Ah, how many Golgothas?
How many, how many Golgothas
Are here on earth for us?
How can we know? How should we know?

Sad, angry, tired: we have kept going,
And reaching the dead-ends of these ordeals,
We have gone beyond them; far beyond
And walked, walked and walked.
Golgotha, Golgotha, African Golgotha!
Africans, black people: Aren't we peculiar?

Ah, what about us?

Ah, what about us?
Some people have a season of sadness,
Then come the seasons of happiness.
Some people have a season of rottenness,
Then come the seasons of flowers.
What about us?
Africans, what about us?

The news from our rural areas is sad.
The news from our towns and cities is sad.
The news from the hills is sad.
The news from the plains and waters is sad.
The news from the forests is sad.
The news from the savannahs is sad.

After rain and deluge takes root a good life.
Africans, what about us?
Africans,
Sadness on everything and everybody falls,
Feeds, plays, sings; and cedes its seat to joy.
Africans, what about us?

The sky turns blue,
The good weather bespatters people with laughter,
New lives spring out and abound around,
Rivers, brooks, lakes with their offsprings
Sing to the world;

Plants wear exuberant clean clothes,
Flowers blossom and fall down never to die,
The leaves' executioners of the previous season
Have turned into angels
And are getting drunk on the flowers,
Competing with the honey's brewers;

Feathered friends in the new clothes are busy
With songs that put more heat
In the trees, in the air;
The breeding moment is a fascinating time
In the life of the creatures in the nature;
Season of abundance! Season of peace!
Season, season of happiness!
Africans, what about us?

Sadness on everything and everybody falls,
Feeds, plays, sings; and goes away;
Then comes peace,
Then comes abundance,
Then comes happiness.
Africans, what about us?

Africans, what about us?
Africans,
Where is our season of abundance?
Where is our season of peace?
Where is our season of happiness?

Each season, each year:
When dictatorships don't deprive us
Of good things that bring a good life,
It is the corruption that gnaws at our lives,
It is embezzlement,
It is well elaborated conflicts
That favor our wealth's theft,
And keep us under big wrong debts,
It is discrimination . . .

Africans,
When are our bright days?
When is our blissful voice in a year?
And you, God, in this deep strange night,
Where are you? Where are your hands?

Africans,
We must bury the terrifying face of fear
And fight for our freedom and progress.
We must bury the terrifying face of fear,
O Africans!

Africa, O my dearest place of birth,

Africa, O my dearest place of birth,
Seized, seized, seized;
Shaken, shaken, shaken;
Abused, abused, abused;
Hit, hit, hit;
Chopped, chopped, chopped;
Pounded, pounded, pounded;
Sucked, sucked, sucked;
Enjoyed, enjoyed, enjoyed.

Africa, earthworm in the ants' teeth!
Africa, bleeding earthworm!
Africa, deer under lions' diamonds!
Africa, O my dearest place of birth!

Africa, O my dearest place of birth,
I want to cry and weep and shed tears
In a manner no human dared before,
I want to honour you with what I have left.

Africa, O my dearest place of birth,
I cry, cry and want to be a new Nile.
I cry, cry and cry . . . alas nothing breaks out.
I forget that this dearest place
Never enjoyed peace in any season;
I forget that it is a place where people
Have tried all the dark fetid things that exist,
And that the past sad swarm of bad events
Did not leave any drop of fluid
In the tired wells of my face;

I hate this litter of life;
I execrate this litter of life
That is the common bread of Africans;
Africa, O my dearest place of birth!
And every time my thoughts are here,
My soul is a rain forest amid which
The heart is a lost sad bird.
They struggle;
They struggle in the night,
They search up and down for the dawn.

We, the people

The African leaders are interesting figures.
Many problems bury their populations
Deeper in the ground, bury and bury,
But the African leaders are proud,
And very satisfied with their records;

Their arrogance constantly unfurls
And shines like the peacock tail.
They feel powerful; they look happy.
But they are houses eaten inside by fires.

They turn their back on the populations,
They take orders, they execute them.
They look at their needy populations,
They know their wants, but look elsewhere.
They have their own interests as priority,
They rule and misuse the populations.

Our people's lives are good ladders that
Our leaders climb to serve their masters,
Climb to serve their brotherhoods,
Climb to serve the friends and themselves.

Our people's lives are brooks that flow
And irrigate our leaders' farms of wealth;
Our people's lives are brooks that flow
And irrigate our leaders' farms of happiness.
African leaders, African lost leaders:

Ah, you'll jump and feed on us and go.
We, the people, we are the water.
We, the people, we are the rough sea.
We, the people, we are here to stay.
African leaders, African lost leaders,
You'll jump and feed on us and go.

He is called Suffering

Africans, the world is full of teachers.
Africans, life is full of masters.
Life and the world abound in advisors.
Life and the world abound in instructors.

But there is only one with great competence.
There is one that is the greatest of masters.
That one comes in second place after God.
Whether we call him advisor or not,
Whether we call him instructor or not,
Call him teacher or not; master or not:

That one comes in second place after God,
And he is called Suffering.
He does not fail any person
That is heedful of her duties,
He does not fail the peoples that really
Pay attention to the life's events.
He never failed them, he never failed them.

Africans,
You who have received a lot from this master
Than the other peoples,
You who have lived with this master
Longer than any other people,
How didn't you learn enough from him?

Africans,
You who did learn a lot from this great master,
How can you remain very naïve?
How can you show such emptiness?
How can you remain in the thick night?

Africans, we are in the fire, in a big fire.
Africans who else can fall into the fire,
Stay still and get used to it as we do?
Africans, isn't amazing, amazing?

Hypocritically

Hypocritically, the rich reject justice,
Hypocritically, the strong delay peace.
The rich get richer as the poor rapidly
Walk back in the deep night of poverty;
The strong get stronger as the weak
Tearfully think of their stolen dignity.

When creepers suffocate young plants,
When a bush is very nasty or disorganized,
How many eyes can see or predict
What will bring back the order?
To anything there is a solution.
Even a lightning sets fire to the bush,
The bush burns down, and new lives sprout.

As things get nasty in the world
And humans stubbornly refuse
To bring a solution to the situation,
Despair and pain capture people's minds.
But it is without knowing what is hidden.
There are many solutions on the way.
One of these solutions is too close.

God's fire pounds the earth's stomach;
The earth cries, cries . . . sheds tears
And squeezes some satanic eggs
That man's hands have cooked
And kept in the laboratories to frighten
And contain the others;
Long darkness, long period of pain,
And the end of it brings a new era.

To anything there is a solution.
Things that humans do not settle,
And settle them in the impartial way,
Destiny takes care of at a given moment,
Using at times the tools we've made.

I found the answer

Like one that has lost something precious,
For many years I walked, and walked
Asking myself these questions:

'Why in the world our African culture
Is not respected or ill-known?
Why is attention not paid to our economy?
Why are Africans not respected in the world?
Why can what is African always suffer?'

And at last,
I looked at the francophone lands of Africa,
And I found the answer.

Today,
I know what nobody knows better than I.
I know that the francophone countries
Of Africa are harems whose owner
Is ferociously jealous and unpredictable;
I know that the francophone counties of
Africa are all gathered and kept on a leash
By a famish greedy master;

As I look at all the following mature women
With all their offsprings and goods:

Algeria, Guinea, Tunisia, Senegal, Congo,
Mali, Niger, Ivory Coast, Burkina, Chad,
Togo, Cameroon, Gabon, Benin, Burundi,
Central African Republic, Rwanda, etc,
All kept on the leash by a tiny noisy master,
I believe that even a dozen of sheep
Can't be obedient to the shepherd to this point;
I find out that with this terrible humiliation,
Their people and cultures can't be respected;

All these mature women follow the master,
They follow him as if they have no teeth;
Aye!

Was I born to witness this humiliation?
To see herds of big zebras cry
And serve under a tiny wild fox?
Ah, leopard's claws in my flesh!
Chest pain, deep chest pain . . . Aye!

Africans,
Herds of zebras are led by a European wild fox;
A wild tiny squirrel has been holding
And pulling a pride in all the filth of earth . . .
Aye!

How could, how can the economy and culture
Of these besieged lands flourish?
How could, how can their people be respected?
Betrayed by his own sons and daughters,
How could, how can Africa wear a dignity?

African people, this is why our sources
Can develop and become great Rivers.

To my questions, at last I found the answer.
African lands have been converted to harems;
Neither the parents nor the children from
The harems thus deserve respect.
Neither the people nor the goods
That are from the harems deserve respect.

Africans,
When the buffaloes are not well organized
And united, they can serve
And suffer for long under the tiniest of mice.

Strange African eyes

When are we going to see?
When are we going to be serious?
Brothers and sisters,
I thought that the lights,
The wrong lit lights limited
Our eyes to see clearly;

Then those fake lights fell down,
(Thanks God!)
And now we stay in the dark.
I was thinking that
From that moment
Our eyes were going to see;

But we behave
As if we were not in the dark still.
We don't see still.
When are we going to see?

We don't see in the dark,
Apparently we will not see
Under the real lights;
When shall we see?

The handful of eyes that see
Are said to be sick or to
Be dangerous to the society.
When are we going to be serious?

The best and the worst places

The best and the worst places of the world;
Where in the world can they be?
Where can we find those places?

We'll go around; we'll tour the world,
We'll find many places and label them.
We may not be sure of the different labels;

And once we come back,
As time sadly or merrily deploys its might,
Amid a succession of events,
We'll make a shocking discovery.

After the same questions to ourselves,
We'll realize that the worst and best places
Of the world are nowhere except in us;
Those places are in us. We are hose places.

The worst and the best places are fully in us.
Mankind, mankind:
Oh the best place of the world!
Mankind, mankind:
The worst place on earth, alas!

The scissors

With all these threads on our minds,
We will never go anywhere.
With the scissors of my words,
I am here to cut the threads that
For many centuries have tied us up;
With the scissors of my words,
I am here to untie a bound people.
I am here to untie the bleeding Africa.
I am here to untie our bleeding land.

The people's future

I believe I know about the people's future.
I know what the people's future looks like.
I know it, I believe I know it.

Knowing a little of the past,
In the present we stand up,
Firmly,
Humbly,
Confidently,
And we don't take our eyes off the future.
We walk and walk towards it, and when
We think we've reached that future,
We notice that the true future awaits us.
If we reach it and sit down,
That means we choose to go back, to die.
Thus is life; we cannot live only the present.

From the back of the present,
We look back,
And ride the horse towards the future;
And that future is always there.
We walk, we walk to it.
As some of us fall down,
We walk to our future that has no end.
Thus is a people's life.
Thus is the challenge of any great people,
Or of any people the path to glory.

O Africa

O Africa my beloved land, tell me:
What are you doing, what are you doing?
Africa who do you expect, expect, who?
Do you count on the foreign help to develop?
Are you expecting the West to liberate you?
Are you expecting the Asians to help you?

Africa, seated enthroned in the night,
You murmur the answer!
You know it is not right
As you disgracefully say,
Yes!
No, Africa!
That will never take place.
No, those people have their own tumors
Growing bigger to worry about; bigger!
Africa, no foreign finger can elevate you;
No foreign finger can liberate you.

Africa, Continent blessed with huge wealth,
Africa, heavy big hive full of honey,
How do you taste, how, how do you taste?
Africa, we, Africans know you are full of honey;
But we don't know, we don't know the taste of it.
Africa, precious hive of the West,
Africa, warehouse of raw materials of the West,
Africa, Africans must liberate you.

Africans, my fellow countrymen:
Under the rains of bullets,
Under the storms of bombs,
Under the clouds of false news,
Under the barks and threats of the UN,
Under the fogs of sanctions,
Africans we must come together
And fight for our independence;
Africans, we must defend our land.

Our African leaders

Ah, Africa, Africa!
Our African leaders have not grown up
To reach the size of a clove of garlic yet;
Even amid them, those we want to trust
End up growing with the roots on the ground,
And the heads kept in the ground.

Ah, Africa, Africa!
Our leaders have converted our land
To a despicable shameful thing;
While other leaders around the world
Fight for their lands and citizens,
Our African leaders weaken us;
And let us with the vultures' dignity.

Our continent has given a lot to its leaders,
But it never reflects the luster
And safety of its cunning leaders;
Our continent has given a lot to the world,
But it never reflects the colors
Of the West that it has built; poor Africa!

Ah, Africa, Africa!
But no matter how filthy and lousy
And poor or sad you can become,
No matter how filthy and lousy
And poor or sad Africans can become,
It is our Africa; we are Africans;
And we don't like any alien hand
That stirs knifes in any of our wounds.

I am the father

I am the father of four children.
I farmed the land to send them to school.
I cared for their health,
I clothed and fed them.
They finish high school,
They went to college and graduated;
Two of them graduated from the university.

I paid for their tuition,
None of them got the scholarship;
As they were successful at school,
Hope and joy hung on their faces
Like abundant fruits that bend the boughs;
As I sacrificed myself for them,
I regarded them as these plants that do
Digest the manures for good results.

Seasons and years came and go,
Weakening my bones and my muscles,
Stealing my strength like leeches at work;
As successes followed their hard works,
I thought that the burdens on my shoulders
Shortly were going to fall down;

As they successfully studied,
I looked and laughed at the killing pain
From bending, selecting, digging, planting,
Sawing, tying, sowing, watering,
Cutting, weeding, reaping, transporting,
Storing and checking along the seasons,
Along the years with the sweltering heat,
With the heavy rain, the cold, the wind;
I thought my burdens shortly would fall down.
Delusion, O delusion!

Studying, they were very ambitious;
Excellent seeds of a country always
Have places on the land to grow
And yield fruits that give pride to the people;
They never farmed the land.
They thought they would be employed
As soon as they would finish studying;

Each of them finished studying brilliantly.
For many years they have been very busy,
They have been busy looking for jobs.
They have been going out at dawn
To return home when the last cocks
Have completely buried the day;

They always came back very tired;
I would ask,
"Children, did you get something?"
Or, "Have you been fed with some hopes?"
And seeing that my questions every time
Were but tools of torture on their minds,
I stopped this disturbing exercise.

Each of my children has had interviews
Thrice the length of the Nile,
And none of them ever got a job.
They are looking for jobs still.
For how long, for how long again?
I don't know, I don't know.

They depend on me still.
The jobs search has stolen their freshness
And kept it to a secret place;
They are young plants that are harshly
Beaten by severe rays of events;
They are very sad, and weary of life.
They'd soon be older than their father.
I am an old bird in cage;
My useless wings cruelly torment me,
I have painted my cage in red;
I have lost my voice; I am lost,
I am excessively served; I am full.

They look at their father with pride
And they tenderly smile; ah sadness,
Their smiles are lights from torn hearts.

And as my eyes control all the fights that
Shyly take place inside their chests
Day after day and week after week,
Month after month and year after year,
(Ah drama of a hard working people)
When there is no rain on the region,
When drought speaks harshly to the region,
And as I can see my broken witty prides,
My eyes provide the farm with enough rain
That makes my plants keep growing.

The children study,
The children are successful,
The children blossom,
But the social order is an invisible wizard
That has changed them to useless fruit trees.

How did we get here?
How did our country get to this point?
One man has led the country to this desert.
He has led the country to this deep filthy swamp.
Amid all these ruins, as if it weren't enough,
Some hands cheer and praise him ardently,
And he smiles with deep satisfaction.

For my unfortunate people, for my children:
I wish that in a single night
Fate slowly walks,
Captures this Calamity of our country,
Gather all his committed supporters,
And buries them all deeper in the ground
Before dawn completely opens its eye;
I finally wish this; I wish it.

As father of four sad children,
As a citizen of a blessed country
Whose people's life is sold or confiscated,
I whish a wave of fatality reaps them all;
I passionately wish it; O I wish it.
I wish it; O I eagerly wish it.

African families

In the African families, life is tough and rough.
Life is tough and rough for the unemployed.
Life is tough and rough for the workers.
Life is tough and rough for the poor.
Life is tough and rough for the rich.
Life is tough and rough for the single and the married.
Life is tough and rough for fathers and mothers.
In Africa, rich and poor live under burdens.

In the African families, there is a sad reality:
On any loaded pair of hands always
Hang many empty mouths;
Any loaded pair of hands is a water point
To which converge almost all the thirsty beings.
This African sad reality has the age of Africa.

Unless things change radically, change
Not at the top, but at the poor families' level,
How can Africa grow and get out of this?
How can this be accomplished?—In many ways;
In many ways, except with the venomous
Proud African leaders who prosper
And are big feeders of the greedy invaders.

In the African families, there is a sad reality:
On any loaded pair of hands always
Hang many empty mouths;
This old sad African reality like a seed
Blew by the winds has crossed the sea
And will take root in the western nations;

Heaven!
Can the westerners understand this change?
Can they (Fragile as they are) accept it as it is?
Can the desperate parents be enough strong
And avoid being but children-murderers?
Can the loaded hands share with the empty?
Can they, would they stand this new reality?
With this new dark day, they may paint
And adorn their societies with blood and fire.
I am praying for the West. I am praying . . .
Africans, let us pray and pray for the West!

They fail to lift Africa up

These African intellectuals who
Speak about and for Africa
And believe they want to liberate Africa,

These African organizations
And associations
That believe they fight
For the continent's liberation,

These African leaders who are up
To sleep or to work irrationally,

These religions in Africa that
Work for mankind's justice and equality:

They have failed and have awfully
Disappointed the African people;
They did not deliver.
They are not delivering.
They must stop feeding on our people.
They must change their methods.
They must change their speeches.
They must revolutionize their approaches.

If that was by ignorance, if it is by ignorance,
It is not late; they should catch up.
But for those who have been leading
And are leading the African people
To the swamps and the seas of poverty,
Of corruption, of disintegration
And of foreign domination:

They must understand that African people
Along the highways of ordeals
Are no longer naïve and stand awake;
They must know that their days are numbered,
They must know that
The ropes are around their necks,
And that African people
Firmly hold these ropes.

The future of our people

Because of them,
The future of our people is in danger,
In great danger; in great danger,
Not because of those who destroy us,
But of those who are at the front on the field
And promise us an imminent victory;
Of all those who know our sores and sorrows
And lie to us that they fight to liberate us.

Because of them,
We are ceaselessly belittled and reified,
We are weighed down with scorns,
We are weighed down with humiliations,
We are weighed down with destabilizations,
And diseases and crimes and wars;
Because of them,
Because of the politicians of the sty;
Yes, in part,
Our people remain here because of them.

Role's change

Nature extremely to mankind was cruel.
As it got blunt and ceased to be so,
Humans took and wore nature's old clothes.
From there until now,
Humans became the big threat to humans.

Our gorgeous House

Our gorgeous House Africa,
Our sacred House Africa,
Acts of pyromania are growing
And flourishing at your doors;
You are on fire; big fire.
Arsonists act and plunder you.
Arsonists set fire to you
And as you ragingly burn,
They throw water drops on you.

Africa our sacred gorgeous House,
Where are your brave men?
Africa, burning looted House,
Where are your firemen?
Where are your warriors?

Africa, in this night of your life,
In this deep night of your history
At this very moment,
Your warriors must come out
If they do exist;
They must come out now,
They must come out to fight,
To help your sun that bleeds heal.

Wealthy empty countries

—The WB and the IMF decide to help us.
African fellow countrymen, beat the drums,
Beat the drums to welcome this good news.
—WB and IMF? That is the saddest of news.
They come to impoverish us;
They come to dictate to us,
They come to enslave us with bad loans
That will put us on the knees.

—Here and there in Africa there are wars,
The UN decides to intervene and bring peace.
African fellow countrymen, beat the drums,
Beat the drums to welcome this good news.
—Ah, just as in Congo with Lumumba,
Just as they intervened in Ivory Coast;
The UN goes to protect the favorite mouth
That favors the interests of some foreign countries;
The UN works for big foreign Corporations,
The UN was born for the oppressors.
Those who send the UN understand the reasons
Of all these wars and know how they end;

—This leader is a good example for Africa.
He does a lot for his country
And he has many good projects for Africa.
He wants his continent freed economically,
He wants it freed culturally and politically.
African countrymen, beat the drums,
Beat the drums to welcome all these good news.

—Ah, poor good African patriot!
His days are numbered; they will remove him
And put in place some mice, some lice
And the populations will experience poverty;
The wealthy country will become empty
And will run into heavy debt.

—They've found some big oil and gold deposits.
The intense exploitation could last thirty years.
Fellow African countrymen, beat the drums,
Beat the drums to welcome this discovery.
—As we know the ruling party,
They will sell that oil very cheap, give it away;
They will let the foreign companies
Take the oil for free to keep for good the power.
The gold is a sweet Coffee
Belonging to the members of the ruling party;
These discoveries could not bring any change.

—They have bought many public buses.
Fellow African countrymen, beat the drums,
Beat the drums to welcome this good news.
—That Tea is for the minister of transportation.
To send people to prison is his favorite game.
Please don't talk aloud about those buses.

—They have built some new stadiums.
Fellow African countrymen, beat the drums,
Beat the drums to welcome this good news.

—Our people venerate sports and games.
As the economies of our countries collapse,
Governors and mayors want to draw and
Push the peoples deeply into sports and games;
They also want to make sure no coins
Remain in the pockets of the poor.

—They promise to build roads and bridges.
Fellow African countrymen, beat the drums,
Beat the drums to welcome this good news.
—Don't forget that the elections are coming.
They know what they are doing.
You'll hear about that in the next ten years,
No steal, no stone will be found at the roadside.

—Here and there they've left mountains of sand
For new schools, hospitals, libraries, parks . . .
This is real; I've seen that; this is effective,
Fellow African countrymen, beat the drums,
Beat the drums to welcome this very good news.
—Houses are safe from now,
Plants are safe from now,
People's eyes are in jeopardy now,
The winds have a lot to fill their stomachs with.
That sand is a good meal for the winds.
For days, for months, for years the winds
Will not suffer from starvation;
They will feed selfishly on the sand
And vomit some cowardly in our eyes.
That is what it is; on them we keep the eyes.

—They recruit and train new soldiers and police,
They build new prisons and police stations,
They buy new weapons and military equipments;
They know that our security is the priority.
Fellow African countrymen, beat the drums,
Beat the drums to welcome this very good news.
—All that to make sure that we lost our mouths,
To make sure that we lose our ears,
Lose our eyes,
Lose our hands and arms
That can harm or disturb them or their sleep.

—Because of long drought this year,
Because of heavy rains and floods this year,
Because of the earthquake this year,
Because of irresponsible strikes this year that
Seriously affect our food production our economy,
We are getting international aid.
Fellow African countrymen, beat the drums,
Beat the drums to welcome this very good news,
—Aid to be given to the families' members,
Relatives and friends of the ruling party;
Aid to be sold on the market as they can't eat all.

—We cannot build the future with pessimism.
—But can lies put bridges on the future?

The African marriages

The route to an African marriage was long,
So long that many pretenders would fail;
The African marriages were the result of
A long process marked by,
Quests,
Investigations,
Patience,
Discretion,
Advices,
And conquest;

There was no physical marriage certificate;
Marriage certificates were written in the air
And inhaled and kept in the hearts;

The western civilization arrived in Africa
With the pen and the paper and contracts
Between men and women stood up,
Left the hearts,
Fled to the papers and majestically sat down;

The western civilization arrived in Africa
With the monogamy and today,
It easily sends some men out
To hide many mistresses everywhere
Like a rat that buries foods here and there
To the point where it forgets some of them,
The foods grow and yield many fruits
And they forget some of them;

The western civilization arrived in Africa
With pleasant soft words which couples
Can now use at home or in public
To cherish each other and show that
That marriage's well even when
It's a falling dam or a broken tree;

The western civilization arrived in Africa
With the kisses in public,
With the birthdays' celebrations,
With the marriages' anniversaries,
With gifts,
With flowers,
With frequent phone calls between the couples,
Even while they commit acts of infidelity;

But coming to Africa,
The western civilization has also cut
And destroyed the roots of the African marriages;
It worsens as the couples live abroad.

Our marriages today are rootless trees.
Our marriages today are real algae
That lively float on the water;
Our marriages today shine like a full moon
In a cloudless sky, like precious gems;
Our marriages today are trees that grow,
Show their beautiful flowers,
And fall down before nurturing their fruit.

Where is thus the strength of Africa?
Our marriages collapse,
Our values are down,
The politics is down,
The cultures are down,
The economies are down;
Everything collapses.
It is the collapse,
It is the collapse everywhere.
I search Africa from east to west,
I search Africa from north to south,
I search Africa on the ground, in the air:
My eyes like an unlucky hunter
Come back empty-handed.
Where is actually the strength of Africa?
What is the pride of Africa?
Where is the pride of Africa?

The hooks to fish us

African patriots, African fighters:
Oh, how many amid us are not the hooks
That the enemies of our countries inside
And outside use or will calmly use
To fish us like fishermen on a rich water,
To divide us like a knife on a big cake,
To tear us out as a pride of lions a buffalo,
To keep us on the ground like a flat
Smooth surface that holds the cockroaches?
How many, how many amid us fight for Africa?
How many amid us rightly serve Africa?
Ah, how many amid, how many amid us
Rightly fight and fall down for Africa?
Africans,
We suffer, we weep, we complain,
We complain and always accuse the others;
We forget that we are the hooks that fish us.

Mines discovery

Mines discovery; smiles,
smokes,
sad squeals.
They take them down; down, down, down
Instead of putting them up, set them free.
Mines discovery . . . mines discovery!

The journalists placed a needle on the sealed barrel
of the new national mines discovery,
they pushed it, pushed it into it and
there was news leak; and the politicians came out.

The first politician talked about the discovery;
the second politician came out and spoke, but
what he told the people contradicted the first;
a third politician had a different tongue,
a fourth had a completely different tongue,
a fifth . . .
a sixth . . .

They all agreed on one thing; the country's building;
they promised jobs to everybody,
they promised to build and equip new hospitals,
they promised to build and equip new schools,
they were going to build roads, bridges, buildings,
they were going to electrify any rural areas,
send free drinking water wherever people lived,
develop and industrialize the agriculture
to move from food importer to food exporter
to feed the Europeans, the Chinese, Indians, Americans . . .
they were going to give free health care
not only to children and elderly people but to all.

In a small town lived a man called Pouockaa;
very educated, he had a Small size prosperous business.
On the lips, comments about the mines discovery
largely outnumbered the amount of dust
that could be found in any harmattan.
As a group of people commented it,
tears escaped from Pouockaa's reddened eyes,
he tried to hide his face
but noticed that it was too late;
his lips trembled, he wept and feverishly said:

"Mines, ah mines! Why did you reveal yourself to us?
rebels' bears grow already on our politicians' opinions;
each of them is the wind of an invisible mentor
and will blow harshly to break any dike on its way;
these natural resources will bring whirlwinds
of impostors to this beautiful quiet land;
big troubles are on the rise on our land,
big troubles knock on the door of my country;
these discoveries will quickly throw this land
in the high waves of hatred and conflicts;
these mines are a bone thrown amid dogs half asleep,
they will awake and fight each other,
but none of them will own it;
it will not benefit the people; it will slip away."

Pouockaa then showed the country as it was
and depicted how it would end in few years.

Before the mines discovery,
there were many villages and tribes living side by side
in harmony, in love and peace;
their lives were a gorgeous cypress of confidence.

After the mines discovery,
the people's life stopped being the same;
it tremendously changed,
it spectacularly changed, changed . . .
(Ah, when the eyes go back to those years,
It is always as if they were the source of the river Congo.)
Everything changed; even the water-courses changed,
waters went rapidly downstream to upstream,
villages were divided, tribes, communities . . .
and inside families, disdainful eyes met
and rocked and poisoned the daily life.

Soft words quickly deserted the politicians' mouths
like the children of the trees under a severe storm;
these soft words could not be heard anywhere;
they were replaced by words-pebbles, words-stones,
words-steel, words-flood, words-storms, words-fire,
words-venom, words-vampire teeth, words-bloodshed . . .
Like a skillful bird that swoops down on its prey,
the discoveries openly slew and took peace away.

The Devil at last had found many customers to whom
He sold the evil to be dumped on the peaceful people.

Hands everywhere already were feeding the evil tools;
big and small sticks, clubs, knifes, machetes . . .
hollow long irons, hollow short irons, thin irons,
big irons, light and heavy hollow irons became the rulers,
and were smoking, spitting burning coals everywhere.

Some people deserted cities and towns and villages
and crossed the country's boundaries as the others
hid in the bushes, swamps, forests or mountains.

Those who fled abroad were like children;
they also experienced want and hatred,
and their souls were but good pipes of homesickness.
To survive men wedded women for whom
They did not have any feeling,
And women found refuge in men they'd never love.

Those who ducked into the nature
And hid were the invaders;
Already they were poor
but they had to pay the rents;
the most expensive rents of life,
those rents were so expensive that
some of the tenants settled there for good,
and could never pay the bills anymore.

Those tenants-invaders owed a lot for their staying
to the beings that owned those places;
they paid a lot to the trap-door spiders,
they paid a lot to the snakes,
they paid a lot to the ants and the termites,
they paid, they paid a lot,
they paid a lot to poisonous plants and fruits;
they discovered the prisons and
the cells of the real hunger;
a hunger that dried out the mothers' milk
and quickly put the babies in the flight,
a thirst that silently sipped people's blood,
a hunger that slowly savored people's flesh,
so they could return Home very light.

As tenants-invaders they learned to live with
Some famous stars and attended
Many unwanted concerts day and night,
and the stars entertained them restlessly.
From the entertainers they bought concerts tickets
with their red wine and as good guests
they were served some delicious dishes of malaria.

African people,
To survive, we have claimed a fruit tree,
But the hyenas have sat beneath it,
And the storm has caught us in the boughs.
How could we ever get down?

Africans something is wrong here;
an unsolved question remains.
How can our resources always become our downs?
How can our morning flowers always
yield dangerous thorns and set fire to the bush?
Why are African children always in need?
Why are they always in need from dawn to sunset?
Something is wrong here, Africans.
There is something very nasty on this land.
Let us sit and look into it closely;
Let us sit, let us sit, and look into it closely.

The underwear of developed countries

Your eyes sadly finish evaluating your country,
And fervently turn to the developed countries.
You gaze at these developed countries;
You gaze at their cities and countrysides,
You gaze at their people admirably
As if you stare at a gorgeous meadow or woods,
(Ignoring all the dirt, mud, thorns, bad insects,
And the poisonous weeds and snakes they shelter)
You gaze at their beautiful long broad roads,
You gaze at their skies full of flying objects,
You gaze at all their infrastructures:

They look as clean as the sloughed snakes;
The dream of living in these countries springs up,
Flows abundantly and floods your mind,
Flows and floods your chest and torments you.
You may do anything for a trip to settle there,
You may lay down everything for a new life there.

You are ready to abandon your job and go,
You are ready to abandon your spouse and go,
You are ready to abandon your offspring
Or even to give away a nursling and go,
You are ready to ruin your family,
You are ready to ruin yourself
Materially,
Financially,
Economically,
Morally,
Just to go, go . . .

But as your eyes scrutinize these countries
Like a hungry eagle the woods and bushes,
You discover the scourges of these countries;
You discover their superficially healed scars,
You discover their putrid wounds,
You discover all their worms:

A significant number of fresh bloods
Of these countries are eaten up by alcohols,
Eaten up by drugs and crimes,
Eaten up by violences within families,
Eaten up by laziness,
Eaten up by sexual lust,
Eaten up by leisures and pleasures;
The populations are eaten up by the governments,
Eaten up by the employers,
Eaten up by discriminations,
Eaten up by poverty,
Eaten up by the videos games,
Eaten up by selfishness, hate, and greed;

These countries are places where the rich
Don't work harder to become richer,
And where by a well set mechanism,
The poor are vast fertile lands
On which the plants of wealth grow quickly;

You stare, stare and stare at all these wounds,
And understand that these places, theses countries
And these peoples are not better off.
You understand that their story of supremacy,
Of security and good life are just the myths,
You understand that they are mirages;
And that you can be better than them,
You learn that you are definitely better than they are.

Dressed appealingly in gorgeous suits,
Many developed countries of this day
Have their underwear full of feces and lice.

If we fall down

In these days, these sad days,
These sad days of our history,

If we fall down in our houses,
History will mock us.

If we fall down in our farms,
History will mock us.

If we fall down doing these jobs
That will never take us anywhere,
History will mock us.

But if our blood kisses the ground
As we move to conquest
And possess our true dignity,
History will glorify us,

If we fall down on the public path
For a common cause,
History will endlessly celebrate us,

And voluptuously call
And tell the future generation
That we stood up bravely
And fell down on the glorious spot.

If we fall down on the right spot,
History will fill our people's ears
With songs-weapons
That will wake them up,
Put them up to fight strongly
And triumph over any aggressors.

If we fall down these days,
It must be on the right spot.

In that blue vampiric shell

African countries,
Third world countries,
What are you doing in that blue vampiric shell
That is used to vandalize your lands,
To conquer and modernly enslave your lands,
To weaken your lands,
To steal your wealth,
To ruin your values,
To create conflicts,
To start wars,
To slaughter,
Massacre,
Genocide your children with such a skill
And innocence that only the vigilant eyes
Can know the bottom of it?

African countries,
Third world countries,
What are you doing?
What are you doing in that wrong shell?
What are you doing in that wrong shell?
What are you doing there
Like people hidden under a rock
Caught in the storm with nowhere to go?
Ah what are you doing there, there?
What are you doing, doing, doing there?
I am amazed, I am amazed.

African countries,
Third world countries,
What are you doing in that boat,
In that boat of domination,
In that boat of discrimination,
And humiliation?
What are you doing there, there?
What are you doing at that place at this time?
I am amazed, I am amazed.

African countries,
Third world countries,
What are you doing at the UN?
What are you doing there?
What, what are you doing there?
Taking the carnivores to your sheepfolds?

What are you doing at the UN?
Taking the carnivores to your sheepfolds?
African countries,
Third world countries,
Irresponsible:
I am amazed, I am amazed.

Dark broody hen

Under a dark broody hen on a neglected land,
There were many appealing big eggs,
There were many appealing big eggs.

Some wild dogs that were on patrol in the wood
Looked at the hen and approached her,
Sniffed at her,
Went and came back and sniffed at her;
And the broody hen remained still.

They barked at her and pushed her . . .
She remained still.
They kept the jaws as if they would promptly
Grasp and crush her head.
She jumped and stood next to her eggs;
One of the wild dogs jumped and seized an egg;
As the broody hen chased the dog,
Another dog stole one, two, three eggs,
The hen returned and chased the dog,
A third dog grasped an egg,
A fourth, a fifth, a sixth, seventh, eighth . . .
The hen cackled, the hen cackled,
Flew and clawed the wild dogs,
Flew and pricked them . . .
A wild dog jumped and seized her feathers;
She escaped crackling and ran away.
The beast spat the hen's clothes,
And rapidly went back to the feast.
The wild dogs ate the eggs, ate the eggs
And wagged their tails,
Ate the eggs, ate the eggs and
Loudly they cried out in triumph.

Not far from the theft scene,
There was another broody hen.
She was glancing silently at her neighbor,
Glancing at her indifferently;
Not far from her there was another hen
That stayed as though everything was normal.

The wild dogs finished the dark broody hen's eggs
And attacked the next broody hen,
And the theft and the fight continued,
And it was similar to the first scene.

A madman who was passing by has stopped.
He had witnessed everything
And insistently he said:

This looks like Africa;
Ah, it is Africa our Africa.
This is Africa the continent of uncertainty,
This is Africa of abundance and of want,
The sole great Rich on earth
That lives in the extreme poverty and misery.
This is Africa our Africa.
This is Africa under my eyes,
As naked as the day it entered the world.
This is Africa, this is our Africa,
Africa from elephant-hope to giraffe-despair . . .
This is Africa far, far behind and
Staying behind and held behind
Like our African women by men;
This, this is Africa;
This . . . this is our Africa,
Our A f r i c a.

This is Africa our Africa,
Naked Africa naked and cold as the sun shines,
Naked Africa naked amid many clothes,
Naked Africa naked shivering with cold,
Shivering with cold amid many clothes,
Naked Africa naked giving its clothes up,
Giving its clothes up to the warmed West!

Naked Africa: is this you, our Africa!
Who could have believed this, our Africa?
Africa you must hold onto your pride
Like the night fly that flies very proud
Of her light beneath the stars;
O Africa!

Beaten,
Bleeding,
Crying,
Completely drowned in our tears,
Voiceless,
Rid of our wealth,

We remain serene,
We remain confident
Very confident under the thickest of nights;
We remain happier than our aggressors.

Africa,
How does this happen?
Strange Africa,
How does this happen?

We cry, they cry

They hurt us; we cry; they cry.
We the victims, we complain,
They, the persecutors complain.
From the day they feignedly cry
As we cry in the night they create.
They can cry and complain;
But the day that their pains
And cries will be true isn't far.
They will bitterly cry from the night.

Tremblingly

Tremblingly they looked at us
And we bent down the eyes;

They first showered some insults on us
And we looked unconcerned;

They gave us some slaps in the faces
And docility shone on our faces;

They greeted us with lashes
And in our childish cries and sobs
They discovered an appeasing music;

They visited us with new diseases,
We rushed to them to cure us;
They greeted us with the rifles
And we knelt down and prayed;

They watered us with bombs
From the planes and are watering us still,
And we waited
And we are waiting for people
That can come and save our lives.

These days they strongly believe
That they know us;
They are all convinced
That we are what we are;

It is a good luck for us.
We hold and hide a great weapon
That all of them ignore.
They think that we are weak
That we are weakened
And that we cannot unite;
They are wrong.

We can kill the virus of treachery in us
And stand as one;
We can kill the virus of egoism in us
And stand as one;
Stand bravely as one.
When we will use these guns
And get use to them:

The imperialist forces will run away;
The vampires' empire will crumble down.
As one,
Africans and world's oppressed people:
Bravely stand!

We can't wait for God

We never take the evil seed of poverty
And sow it in the other nations' ground.
But our lands are full of sequoias of poverty;
Our lands are full of baobabs of indigence.
We don't know how the machines guns
And the bullets are made;
But our bodies are good shelters for them,
And they decorate our lands with our fleshes.

We don't know the horrible bombs' ingredients,
No, we don't know, we don't know
the horrible chemical weapons' ingredients,
we don't know them,
But all these weapons are around us.
They surround us and woo children lives,
Woo adults' lives, woo innocent's.
We have wealth that brews abundantly
And serves us the darkest of nights on earth,
Our lit firewood burns but release the cold,
Our blankets are colder than a slab of ice.

We can't talk of fate in our tragic situation.
We can't wait for God;
God has nothing to do with our tragic lot.
We must keep God away from this case.
The Master can't be invite to this matter.
If we dare to wait on Him,
We will be all dead before His arrival.

I come here very humbly, to unveil
And show the true face of the God
We wait for as ordeals hold us down.
That God wait quietly in us,
That God is:

Our Actions in Discipline with Confidence.

This is the true God,
The true God we've been waiting for,
Waiting in tears,
Waiting in pain.
As long as we remain in these conditions,
This must be our true God,
And the only one.
We must not be frightened.

Nothing should frighten us.
The supreme hands hold sophisticated weapons
That they don't want us to build or possess;
They have strong armies.

We don't need sophisticated weapons,
We don't need strong armies.
We need strong minds to defeat them all.
To defeat them all,
The passionate love of our lands,
And our intelligent actions are enough.

Parents, adults and friends,
Tell the children our history and our situation.
Each one must grow up soldier,
Each oppressed head must be a soldier,
And know that he or she belongs naturally
In the army of the oppressed;
Know that his or her army's an isolate act
That avenges his or her humiliated country
Or avenges the reified Africa;

To get back our full dignity,
We don't need any strong army,
We can't wait for God.
Our lives have always been in danger;
To be safe and free, we must live dangerously.

We need strong minds to defeat all them.
We can't wait for God.
If we the oppressed understand these truths,
Our victory will hasten to come
Like a young bamboo plant that runs in the air.

About my dances, my clothes

I

About my dances,
About my African dances,
They insist they don't like them
And call me uncivilized man;
But I refuse to give in.

About my clothes,
About my African clothes, my hat and jewels,
They insist they don't like them
And call me uncivilized man;
But I refuse to give in.

About my foods,
About my African foods,
They insist they don't like them
And call me uncivilized man;
But I refuse to give in.

About my gait,
About my personal gait,
They insist they don't like it
And call me uncivilized man;
But I refuse to give in

About my smile and laughter,
About my African smile and laughter,
They insist they don't like them
And call me uncivilized man;
But I refuse to give in.

I look at them and laugh the way
I always laugh;
I love to laugh as a big fire on the bush,
And they say I am a primitive,
They ask me to hide my uvula
As I laugh,
They ask me to hide my molars
As I laugh,
They ask me to hide my tongue
As I laugh;
I laugh like the hippopotamus
That is involved in a fight,
Laugh as a chick
That gets food from its mother.
And I let them know that
Their rules and codes frighten me.
But I refuse to give in.

But all this is nothing.
It is nothing compared to
The air strikes they drop on my soul.
They pound it with heavy words,
But I refuse to give in.

The air strikes do not come
As they accuse me of trying to
Africanize the modern dances
When I stand up and dance;

The air strikes comes after
They surprise me many times
Eating with the bare hands,
Turning my fingers to forks,
And my hands to spoons;
They become furious;
I am not talking of the Westerners.
I talk of my African brothers and sisters.
They pound me with heavy words.

It worsen as I exercise my rights
This year at a big party;
Each one has a spoon, a fork,
A glass and a knife;
Clothed in the African fashion,
I have mine by my plate too.
But I ignore them.

My right hand sinks into the plate
And catches as much food as they can
And it vanishes into my mouth.
My left hand seize my bottle
And its mouth finds refuge into my mouth;
My fingers like a pair of pliers
Hold the meat and my teeth cut it.

My African brothers and sisters publically
Call me uncivilized man.
They say I am far behind,
Some call me animal,
Others eye me with eyes-storms and say
I remain in the rainforest of civilization,
They say I eat fast and nastily like a pig,
And another fingering me say: No, no
This is a pig, this is a wart hog.

I ignore these rules and bylaws that
Rid our society everyday of what we are.
I understand that if I let them
Advance until my kitchen and win,
I have nothing left,
And serve them the best of what
The wild beast has;
And I can hear repeatedly here and there:
"Who did invite the beast here?"

As I finish my meal,
I tell them that my hand remain
The best spoons and forks ever invented;
I tell them that when I eat
It is the only way
I have a good appetite,
Pleasure and joy;

Drowned in a deep pond of anger,
They can't listen to me;
They are but dogs chasing a game.
They are big fires on a huge bush.
I think that it is madness and I laugh.

I ask them to be tolerant,
But they don't listen.
I tell them that my fingers-forks
And my hands-spoons don't harm anybody,
I tell them that my laughter-volcano and
My smiles-earthquakes do not wound anybody;
I ask them to be tolerant
That it is my right,
That it is my right,
And I cry out:
My right, my right . . .
But they don't want to listen

I imagine we are in a doomed day,
They may all die by a food because
They can't eat without folks, spoons, knifes . . .
They may all die because they are civilized.
O poor God creatures!

II

After the incident at the big party,
A friend that always understands me
Has a party and invites many people.
They can voluntary bring some foods and drinks.

I prepare a traditional food from my native land
To be eaten with a special sauce;
A sauce that is as sticky as the glue.

Once all the guests are in,
I promise to change my African way,
At the condition that some volunteers
Accept my meal and finish it
(Using the forks and spoons)
At the same time I do or before me,
Or just a short while after me;

We equally share it and start eating.
Within six minutes mine is finish.
Ten minutes . . . are still struggling;
Fifteen minutes . . .
Twenty minutes,
Thirty,
Fifty . . .

And they were before their plates,
Struggling, struggling with their foods,
Striving to
Get a portion of the sauce to the mouth.
They are confused,
They breathe faster,
They sweat.

My friend puts an end to the torture.

I look at them
And ask them to learn to be tolerant.
I tell them,
I have a way to
Laugh and smile
When joy grows and bursts in my chest;
I have a way, my way to
Eat,
Dress,
Dance,
Walk . . .
It is my way and the good way
I love.

I tell them:
If you force me
And I have to
Stop laughing, smiling, dressing,
Eating, dancing and walking
The way I grew up doing,
Isn't a big part of my life I throw away?

Isn't my life thus becoming a boneless meat
That is thrown to a big healthy dog?
If I cannot laugh the way I love to laugh,
Is it not to turn my laugh to this boneless meat?

You ask me to deny myself!
It is suicide, and I hate suicide.
Ah people don't do that to me,
Don't do that to me . . .
Let me be me; be me, be just me.
You are liars,
I won't let you destroy me.

My culture is my head.
I won't let you touch it.
My culture is my shell.
I won't live out of it.
If I desert my culture,
I will face the pitiless rain
Or sun of instability,
Of dizziness,
Of being from nowhere
And will be turned to nothingness;

My culture is my fortress.
If I decide not to live it and leave it,
I am lost;
I am a bird in the sky
That plunges into a burning bush.

The bloodthirsty angels

They live fearless like lions in the bush.
In their society, except natural threats,
Children and parents, friends and relatives,
Individuals and couples; singles and
Married people all don't live under attacks.

Whether they are in their homes or away,
Their lives are not threatened.
They go to the stores, to the markets
To buy or sell or have fun,
And their lives are not threatened.

They go to the restaurants to the clubs,
They go to the stadiums to the operas,
They go to the parks to play,
To play leisurely; to play intensely,
And their lives are not threatened.

They go in the woods and spend the day;
They go by bikes by cars, by buses by trains;
They go to the beach; they go on the boats,
On the ferries
On the rivers on the sea and the lakes,
And their lives are not threatened.

They go everywhere and
They are always fearless.
They go in peace,
Stay in peace,
Go back in peace;
Their countries don't have civil wars,

Their countries are not under any attacks,
Their countries don't know wars.
Their lives are not threatened.

In our world that is but a rain forest,
The common people of these countries live
Like the subterranean creatures of the forest.
They ignore the heavy rains and the torrents
That pound and pound the forest;
They ignore the frightful nights of the others,
Invented deep nights,
Intentional nights forged by their leaders.

They ignore the mosquitoes that are away
And live on the blood of the forest's creatures;
They ignore the drought, the storms, the cold,
The lightening that hit and weaken the forest;
Their lives are not threatened.

The common people of these countries
Know very little about their governments.
They know very little about their practices.
They often ignore the sickness of their countries.
They often ignore the crimes and sins
That their governments leave on the body of
Many countries and on the people's minds;
They know that their governments are the lambs
And ignore that they banks robbers, gangsters,
Fires raisers and the worst terrorists of the world;
As they live in peace and breathe peace,
They often ignore these things.

They ignore the different wars waged
By their governments over the world
For wealth and strategic points' control;
They ignore about the bloody unjustified wars,
And when they know about them,
They naively accused the victims of barbarities,
Of atrocities, of human rights' assailants;

They ignore all about the children
Of the other countries whose lives
last night,
This week,
Last week,
last month,
last year,
two years ago,
a decade or
many decades ago,
Have been stolen by well orchestrated conflicts,
Have been stolen by the machines guns,
Have been stolen by many heavy bombs
Thrown from the warplanes or the warships;

They ignore the untold or partial told stories
Of some families' members: children, parents,
Sisters, brothers or relatives who have been
Allegedly sent abroad to defend their countries,
Though they went there and put at risk their lives
For the interests of some businesses groups;

They ignore that often some of these veterans
Start their stories and become just very weak
To count them because the stories are frightful;
Because their true stories strangely are stories
Beyond the stories that can be told.

Ah these veterans can never have the nerve
To sit down and count the true stories of the crowds
At which they pointed the machines guns
From a street corner or from the warplanes
And the guns' spittle flattened them in great number
Like a rough storm that visits a banana plantation;

They can never have the nerve to count the stories
Of the innocent families bombed in the houses;
Or the ones of the houses set on fire the way
Nobody could escape; and heard the 'Woy,
No, hay, woy wey, hee, heee, hoho, wooo,
Woo, no, humm' rock the house, rock the air,
Rock their ears . . .
. . . Followed by a big wave of silence . . .

Then, the 'Boom, boom, peuf, boom peufff!
Boom boom, boom peupeuff, booom!' that
Fed the air, fed their ears, besieged their souls,
Sealed the exit and would stay there forever,
And they knew very well that
Those were the parents' cries and stomachs,
And they knew very well that

Those were the children's cries and stomachs,
And they knew very well that
Those were the cries and stomachs of the elders;

How can they ever count the stories
Of the innocent lives taken in the cold blood
When they could not find the suspects?
No; they can't suffer atrociously many times.
They can never go back and climb all these trees
And mountains of pains and shames;
Forever they choose to suffer and
Die consumed little by little by these secrets.

The common people of these countries
Ignore the houses, the schools and hospitals
Of the others destroyed by their governments,
They don't know at all about the railways,
Roads and airports destroyed by their countries,
They ignore all about the means of transport
Of the others that were pounded by their bombs,
They don't know about the children-soldiers
Killed or who killed, paid by their governments;

They ignore all about the seeds of insecurity,
The seeds of poverty, of modern form of slavery
That their countries have selected and knowingly
Sown in the soils of the others and which nowadays
Yield some gorgeous fruits of disasters;
They ignore all about the illegal bad medical tests
Done on the naïve children of the other countries;

They ignore all about the killings of the poor
By the invisible powerful bombs prepared and
Thrown by the very kind IMF and the WB;

They ignore all these crimes and sicknesses
Of their governments or businesses groups,
And know only what they pretend to be.

With these generations of physically wounded,
With these generations of morally wounded,
With all these traumas from parents to children,
From generation to generation,
How should peace ever water our lives' paths?
How should these atrocities ever desert our skulls?
How should we ever live a quiet and peaceful life?
Wherever we turn, we see the bloodthirsty angels.

But the way things go these days,
With the arrogance of some strong nations
Of the world overfilling the cup,
Behind the African and Mediterranean nights
I read the coming of the world's deep night.

This piece of shame

Power, power,
Rid of wisdom,
Rid of honour,
Rid of marrows,
Rid of bones:
Bitterness is brewed
And is left to be taken;
But they ignore the taste of it still.
They contemplate it
And smile;
They rejoice
To have the power
And to rule;

But what is it worth, this empty thing,
This rotten stinking flesh,
This piece of shame that
They hold very arrogantly?

To get this piece of shame,
They harvest people's breaths
Like busy farmers who fill
Baskets with bunches of grapes;

No wisdom, no honour,
No marrows, no bones:
Is this power which in essence
Aims to improve lives' quality?

Living abroad

Living abroad, I discovered a new life.
That discovery was a meal that I could
Not keep selfishly;
I love to share, I love to share.
I am going to give it away; give it away.

On my first days when I left the house,
I would stop and greet people;
Greet them naturally,
Talk to them naturally.
But I witnessed amazing things.

Strange smiles came on their faces.
Some stormy honeyless smiles;
How could smiles light people faces
And just after one second bitterness
Came and kingly nested on their faces
Like wasps' nests on the trees?

I went and came back to the house,
Seriously tortured by what I saw.
I thought those smiles were artificial.

The next day, I greeted my neighbor
Naturally, very naturally and said
That I was an Africa's pure blood;
He smiled artificially;
His heart became a fertile thing.
From his lips escaped artificial words
Like bullets from shining machines-guns.

The following day I saw him again.
He was living a big house alone.
Alone; I saw nobody visit him
For days, weeks, months . . .
He was alone like the selfishness.
I saw him and again I said, Hello!

That day died and the next day
I saw him again at the same place,
And dropped him a honeyed smile;
He didn't like it; he didn't like it at all.
He asked me what I wanted.
I wanted to know if I needed help.

Heavens knew that I did not need help.
I was toiling and getting all I needed.
What I needed was a deep smile.
What I needed was a natural smile,
A true smile I was used to,
A true smile of the traditional Africans,
A smile escaping from the heart
Like a spring water from a clean ground.

I was looking for life,
Not life in the loneliness;
I was looking for life,
Life that is but inlaid in the community.
I grew up in an African society where
A lonely bee in the hive has no life;

Living abroad, I discovered a new life.
I surprisingly discovered that one person
Could be a family though she was alone,
Though she had only a cat as companion;
I amazingly discovered that one person
Could be a whole community,
Could be a whole town,
Could be a whole city,
Though she was alone or only had a dog.

I discovered a new life living in the West.
Ah, enough to see bad things flourish.

I saw these things in the first years,
And they disappeared,
They vanished tough they were around,
But not around for me;
The habit kicked them out of my sight.

We must not love the pain

We endure suffering and pain.
We know how to stand the pain.
But we must not love the pain.
Where are we?
Ah, does it not look like
We bear the pain
At the point we love it!
We have had it as friend for so long . . .
On our thresholds,
On our gray hairs,
On our minds,
On our Nile-eyes,
On our backs,
On our shoulders,
Chests,
Hands,
Fingers,
Thighs,
And knees as we go down to say:
Yes Sir!
We have had pain as friend for so long,
And this keeps us in the nights.

Because of it

Because of it, all over the world,
Humiliation is the stubborn
Great companion of the Blacks;

It follows them. They budge,
It follows them, follows them.

They look before,
They see humiliation smilingly
Wait on them like a vile whore;

They look behind,
They see it follow them as their shades;

They turn left, they see it
Run into them like a vile whore;

They turn right,
it smiles at them generously
And naturally like a baby;

They look up,
They see it come down onto them
Like the fastest of birds of prey;

They turn their eyes to the ground
To rest after getting all the moral
And physical wounds of earth:

They feel humiliation on the ground,
They feel humiliation under their heels,
They see humiliation smile at them,
They see humiliation hold their feet,
They see her kiss and leak their feet.

Because of their skin,
All over the world,
Humiliation is the stubborn
Great companion of the Blacks;

They have a different rate everywhere.
They have a different justice everywhere.
Their fines are always the highest,
Their treatments are always the worst,
Their jail times are always the longest;

To appear at last on the merits lists,
They must work till their hairs turn gray,
They must do twice or thrice
What others skins have done;

In any occasion when they are suspects,
They can be followed and investigated
Ten times longer than the other skins.
Humiliation, humiliation . . .
Humiliation is the Blacks' good friends.

Blacks, Blacks where are the black leaders?
Who shall ever mend your broken hearts?
Where do these strong hands hide now?
Where are they, as you're turned upside down?

Blacks, Blacks, Blacks
These truths are but killing pains;
Blacks, I always feel so sorry for you.

Mighty law

There is a mighty law on earth.
There is a mighty law on earth,
A mighty law to be followed,
And that mighty law is for all:

Plants, humans, animals, things,
Individuals, communities, nations,
Small, big, weak, strong;

There is a mighty law on earth,
A mighty law to be followed
That can be summed up in these words:

Birth, growth, apogee and fall;

Arrogant and stubborn as volcanoes,
Some individuals, some groups,
Or nations seek to be above this law.

There is a powerful western nation
That remains the most zealous amid them;
The authorities of this country strongly
Believe that their filthy criminal acts
Around the world as in their own Home
Can keep their country above this law;

The leaders of this collapsing powerful
Western nation believe that to go around,
And disturb and destroy the finances and
The economy of some developed
And weak countries will save their country
From sinking; it is unstoppable.

This collapsing gigantic nation is ready
To wound the whole world to stay up;
This collapsing powerful nation is ready
To set the whole world on fire to survive;
This collapsing gigantic nation is ready
To wage a nuclear war against its creditors
To never pay its huge frightful debts;

Already, humanity's absent from its mind;
More ferocious than the Barbarians of yore,
This nation and its friends work restlessly
To carry away spoils from here and there
To escape the threatening teeth of poverty;
Ah, fragile timorous nation!

Great civilized nation, you kill, kill
Kill the brothers and sisters and go free;
You kill the children and patriarchs
And go, come back and kill and go free;
You break, weaken, emasculate and steal . . .

No; learn to deal with the reality and truth.
Clever face, crooked face: how long,
How long will you keep running wrongly?
Be responsible, O coward powerful nation!
You must follow the law,
You must follow the law:
Birth, growth, apogee and fall;

He who seeks everlasting Eden on earth
Will plunge and sink into everlasting Hell.

Greedy officials

Greedy officials,
Greedy, greedy they are.

Their greed makes deep holes
Into our economy,
Into our values
Like worms that go and
Build boulevards into the fruits.

Like October breeze
That claims the life of leaves
Slowly one by one
Till the trees stand naked,

Instead of working
To develop the land,
They live like locusts
On the farm of vegetables;

They harvest the country
Little by little,
Little by little,
Till the rich country
Lies down
Like a giraffe's carrion
After lions' great feast;

Greedy officials,
Greedy, greedy they are.

Many times our people
Have launched grief
Into the nations' ears,
But as answer,
High larva of silence
Have rocked their eardrums,
And they even have caught
These nations talk hand
In hand with their oppressors;

Greedy officials,
Greedy, greedy they are.

Cunning sadistic officials,
Cunning sadistic nations;

Ah people, strange sauce!
Sauce that has been used
On all the world's foods!
The world is a wood of hypocrisies.

And every time
I gaze at our land,
Our land infested and
Filthier than a swamp,
I wonder how we got
Trapped in this mud at this point;
O majestic perennial sorrow
Of our peoples!
Why can men do this to men?

Greedy officials,
Greedy, greedy they are.

Amid this stench,
We will not let the light
Of our mind go off;
On this rottenness,
We must plant some trees.
Rottenness, rottenness, rottenness:
Rottenness is the tree for future flowers.

The future of the world

Often when we look at the world,
Look at the plants at the rivers,
Look at the lakes at the oceans,
Look at the natural resources,
Look at the wind at the sun,
Look at the natural marvels,
Look at the modern wonders,
Look at the world's wealth:

Suddenly we feel happy to be here,
To grow and live here on earth,
Here on this pleasant planet earth,
To be part of this paradise;

And then when we stare at peoples,
When we glance at the daily events,
When we peer at people's activities,
We see here and there many seas
And bushes of cruelties rise around us,
We find ourselves defenselessly
Caught In the heavy chains
Of a handful of unscrupulous minds;

Suddenly we get the truth like the deer
That stands at a meter from a cheetah,
We henceforth know where we live,
Our planet's beauty rapidly melts
Like the beeswax brought to the fire.

But knowing what we are losing
Or what we have lost,
We refuse to give up and stand up.
We refuse to sleep, refuse to let the lice
Invade and own this planet.

And to these lice that firmly believe
They are the world's masters,
We recall this:

World's masters,
The bitter leaf will abundantly fall
Onto your sweet salad plate
No matter what you do;
World's masters,
No matter what you do,
The world will at last be a free world.

World's masters,
This world has never been our world,
It's not the world of all for all.
We are absolutely convinced
That a one-head-world leads to disasters,
A one-head world leads to chaos,
It puts many nations in the slavery farms,
The world to be free must not have one head.
But we know this, come what my,
The world will at last bee a free world.

We are not talking of the fake free world
That you promote and extol;
We are not talking of the world
Of selfishness and injustice that you build;
We talk of a free world rid of artificial gods.

These artificial gods that can destroy
Anything they want, kill who they hate;
These gods that elevate who they want
And crush those they don't control;
These gods that have the power
To tell what is wrong what is right,
Tell what is dark what is bright;
These gods that take the sun down
And put darkness up,
Put the sun up and take it down,
Create the season of abundance,
The season of starvation;

The world has no spot for them.

World's masters,
The world does not need artificial gods,
The world does not need you, want you;
The world will at last be a free world.

They never get the right thing

Because they never get the right thing,
They decide to stand and get everything.
They decide to get everything,
Not gently,
Not convincingly,
Not persuasively,
But forcedly, wildly, cruelly,
Because they are drunk on their blind might
That advises them not to be clever wooers.

They decide to abduct
And kidnap the world;
They decide to be the world's owners,
They act like the world's owners,
They think they are the world's owners.

Their long defying teeth feel dull
And sink into my mother Africa,
My mother Africa bleeds and withers;
For gems and mines in the Africa's body,
They are ready to crush all the children.

They decide that none of the children
Ever shall breathe,
And that they'll never rest themselves,
Unless their knife opens Africa's stomach,
Open all her veins, and get all;
Get all what can keep Africa alive strong.

Because they never get the right thing,
They decide to stand and get everything.
And they remain empty, miserable, lost.
Ah, poor world's owners!
They shall never rest, never . . .
It is a curse.
Africans, remember!

If only I could call back the time

When I see what Africa has come to,
When I see the daily events in Africa
And what has been happening for decades,
I think of its great figures that have travelled.

If only I could call back the time,
I would promptly call it
Knowing that it would come back
With Samorry,
Sankara,
Touré,
Nkrumah,
Nasser,
Lumumba,
Fanon,
Cabral,
Nyerere,
Um Nyobé,
Khadafy . . .
Potent African symbols of liberation!

If only I could call back the time,
I would promptly call it
Knowing that it would come back with
These figures and they'd be amazed
To see the cowards that rule upon Africa
And eagerly want to be respected.
They'd be amazed to see the traitors
And the torturers that paralyze Africa
And want to be venerated.
Ah, if only I could call back the time!

The more we talk peace

Africans,
The more we talk of peace,
The more they reify and hit us.
The more we are nice to them,
The more we are humiliated and slain.

What are we going to do of all these bodies?
Isn't silly to follow Gandhi for ever
And never get our rights back?

Knowing that the way is short
And that we get what we want
By lining up decisively behind Little:
Isn't that to act responsible?

Our lands are strewn with bodies;
What are we going to do of these bodies?
And they keep falling, falling.
To follow Gandhi, are we not but silly?

Water hole

World bigger water hole;
Many deadly battle fields wittingly planned
And started around it by some hands;
Friendly or not,
Peaceful or not,
These hands are around to open
And close their claws on their preys.
World bigger water hole!
Where is it on the face of the earth?
What is this water hole's name?
In Africa of course;
Africa of course;
It cannot be elsewhere.
It cannot be a different name.

Young men

Nobody understands young men nowadays.
Nobody understands them; nobody.
They are not like the young men of the past.
They are always like a severe diarrhea.

The young men of today are very quick;
And quick people don't often get things right.
Unlike the cheetahs that target well
And near their preys before hunting them,
Young men of today,
Ah young men, young men!
They stand and without seeing clearly,
Suddenly they rush towards their target
And collapse as they are short of breath.

Young men, young men of today!
They are not patient as those of the past.
Nobody knows how they will end;
Nobody knows.

In the past when a mouse approached
And gnawed stealthily at the meal
That belonged to a young or old married man,
He would stare calmly at his dish,
Sorrowfully shake the head and say:

"Now, what can I do to change what is done?
Nothing . . . it's too late . . . what is done is done.
There is nothing I can do; thus is life."

Then he would jealously keep his meal and
Continue to eat it; eat it, gluttonously eat it,
And would proceed to his self-criticism and
Think that he was partly responsible.

But this day young men hate this path;
They walk far away from this path; they hate it.
This day when a mouse scratch a meal,
The young man just throws it away and
Eagerly looks for another one.

Nobody understands young men today.
The life of young men today's a disaster.

Dominated Africa

Why do they dominate us?
They don't dominate us at this point only
Because they master sciences and technologies;

They don't dominate us at this point only
Because they remain militarily stronger;

They don't dominate us at this point
Because they are smarter than us;

They dominate us because we never stop
Believing that they are friendly and helpful;
They dominate us because we think they care;
They dominate us because we see them superior;
They dominate us because they look at us
And find that we are selfish and divided;
They dominate us because we hate ourselves
And know them shallowly;
They dominate us because they know us
As people that have only faith in Providence;
They dominate us because we've chosen
To stay stubbornly in the blanket of naivety;

Africans, we are behind because they exist.
They dominate us because we want it so.
All men are created free;
We must learn to ignore any being
That's resolutely a dyke to our freedom.
They are dead in my consciousness.
Africans,
Kill the dominators in your minds and live,
Live a full life,
Live a new flourishing life.

Ineffaceable scars

We cover them with laughing and smile,
And we keep them; we keep all our scars;
And nothing can wash and remove them.
We keep our scars, we keep all them.

For justice that must be for all,
For freedom that must be for all,
Chris Hani and Robert Sobukwe fought,
Fought and served their breathes;
Scar, ineffaceable scar!

For justice that must be for all,
For freedom that must be for all,
Steve Biko and unknown men and women fought,
Fought and served their breathes;
Scar, ineffaceable scar!

For justice that must be for all,
For freedom that must be for all,
The children of Soweto fought
And generously served their breathes;
Scars, ineffaceable scars!

For justice that must be for all,
For freedom that must be for all,
Nelson Mandela fought
And went to Robben Island
And went to Pollsmoor;
Scar, ineffaceable scar!

He went there; he was lucky;
He was lucky and stayed longer,
And at last saw the sun;
Some did not stay long and left,
Left freed or were devoured,
Were devoured by the sharp
Strong teeth of torture of the artificial gods;
Scars, ineffaceable scars!

We cover them with laughing and smile,
And we keep them; we keep all our scars.

Robben Island, Soweto and Pollsmoor . . . ah,
Indelible marks on the African skin!
Leopards that hunt us day and night!
Horrible eternal ghosts amid our lives!

Robben Island, Soweto, Pollsmoor:
Scars on our souls,
How can we ever forget you?
No tsunami, no earthquake, no storm,
No volcano can ever take you down.
We Africans we live with you,
Forever you are in us;
And here and there on our lands,
We continue to get more every year.

Prisons swallowed many souls,
Weapons swallowed many souls,
Artificial gods sowed violence,
Artificial gods sowed poverties and fears
To keep Blacks in the chains of the shades;

But in the end,
In the end the laws and the weapons
Of the artificial gods could not
Continue to feed on the oppressed anymore.

An unforeseeable light shattered the shades,
And partially set the victims free.
They would learn to walk
And become completely free.

In that country,
The gods emasculated the might of terror
That they used and were building,
The might that their peers
Have been using all over the world
To maintain the Weak to the ground;

They made sure Mandela was a sheep,
They made sure he was a hornless ram,
They made sure he could not bite them,
And they released and put him up.
He did not bite them;

He did not bite them; but if the sun
Does not come down on all those Blacks,
Someone else would go up there,
Seriously bite them and the traitors mortally,
And
The rays of sun would come down on all.

We keep all our scars; we keep them.
And carefully,
We cover them with laughter and smile.
We keep all our scars; we keep them.

We are not lazy

Africans,
The West knows we are not lazy.
We Africans know we are not lazy.
Our real problem is the rope around us;
We Africans cannot take off with it.
To fully pace the street of freedom,
We need the key of the gate to this street.
We know that the West keeps this key.

Africans,
But never the West will give us this key.
Our kindness, our bounty, our fairness,
Our love, never can just give us this key.

But we Africans,
Though at time we behave like ignorant,
We know where the real right key is,
We know we know we know where it is;
We hold the real right key; we have it:
It is to walk decisively, consequently,
And harshly to grasp our freedom;

We must walk decisively, consequently,
And harshly to end the long game;
They show us leaves we show them leaves;
They show us steels, we show them steels;
The defecate on us, we defecate on them;
They urine on us, we pay them back twice;
Our women become their favorite tools,
We nicely treat their women like doormats.

We hold the real right key; we have it;
It is to walk decisively, consequently,
Maturely and harshly to grasp our freedom;

Make the child Equality painfully wail,
And bring us and them together at last,
Together as good brothers and sisters;
Not to do this, is to lack respect to Equality.

We are not lazy, we are not weak,
We need to be free;
We must stand and do it ourselves,
And feed Equality that remains empty.

The hunters

The first time hunters visited the Continent,
They did not know too much about it;
They did not know that its stomach was full of riches.
Since they knew about it and were desperately in need,
The hunters are back like hungry hyenas resolute
To have a good piece of meat from the African game,
Even if each of them may lose an eye, a tooth or a leg
In these fights they are seldom the losers.

The hunters are back like hungry hyenas;
And because the African bush is not united,
Any African who stops the hunter from shooting
Even the tiniest of squirrels may lose her arms,
Lose her legs,
Lose her eyes,
Lose her ears,
And
Easily may lose her life.
Ah, gloomy flowers,
Gloomy flowers of African natural resources!

And when I lift my tearful eyes on the hunters' faces
And look for a reason to forgive them,
My poor eyes don't fall onto any remorse.
I don't see any guilt in their arrogant eyes.
When I lift my tearful eyes on the hunters' faces,
I see some vivid lit lamps of hate in their eyes,
Lamps that shine as if to tell us that
We haven't seen anything yet.
Ah nights, nights, perennial African nights!

Africans,
Behind the handful of Africans who clearly see
The complexity of our situation and can courageously
And successfully bring some solutions to it,
Behind these sons and daughters
Who are up, and are resolutely up:
Africans stand up firmly!
Africans support the cause!
Support the cause and the cause will smile at us.

Africans again

Again in 2011 at the UN, it happened.
By embracing the 1973,
Three Africans confirmed
That Africans remained good guinea pigs;

They used Africans at the UN Securityless Council
To move and break the African spine;
They used Africans as usual to hold
And control and destroy the poor Africa;

They promised the three Africans some cheap junks
As they did in the traditional slavery days,
To plunder and emasculate the wealthy Africa;

They used Africans at the Securityless Council.
They keep doing to Africans
The same thing they did to Christ,
And Africans still let them do what they
Let them do long ago;

They do the same thing they did to Christ to us.
They did not embrace Christianity for Christ's sake.
They jumped and kissed Christ
And used Him in Africa as a cruel tank,
Used Him as a cruel tank in America,
Used Him as a cruel tank in Australia,
(A tank used to steal, cause sufferings and deaths.)
Tried to use Him in Asia but it faced resistance,
Tried to use Him in the Middle East and failed;

Those who let them bring Him in,
Or were forced to let Him in,
All those peoples have seen the hell.

Learn to be ready

You say that you can be a great farmer;
You can become
what you want.
You say that you were a great farmer;
You could become
what you wanted.
You say you want to be farmer again.
You can become
what you want.

But you say you are amid a severe drought.
You say that around you there is no water.
Ambitious hand,
Have you ever been that farmer?
O heart filled with unhappiness,
Can you ever be that farmer?

You are ready like a child
Your land is a bush still,
And you are waiting for the rain.
Your land is a bush still,
And you are blaming the rain.

When rain comes,
What will you do, how will you be?
You'll run in all directions,
You'll be very confused.
In life, learn how to be ready.
In life, don't be reactive. Be proactive.

Lost children

Our children, children we know you.
Our children, lost children, we know you.
We know you, we know you;
We know what is taking place in the cities.

When you come here in the village,
Don't come home with the cities,
Leave the cities behind you,
And be in the village with the village.
Our children, children we know you.

In the village, we are always real,
We are always fair, we are authentic.
When you come to the village,
When you come to see us,
When you are here in the village,
Make sure that you wear the village smile.
When you are coming in the village,
Please keep the cities in the cities,
Keep the business smile in the cities.
Leave them there, leave them there,
As you tread upon our clean land.

Don't come here with the make up smile.
Be natural, be sincere,
Be sensitive and flexible.
Let your smiles be the flowers of your hearts,
Let your sadness speak for their bitterness.
Our children, lost children, we know you.

Where was the world, where is the world?

South Africa, South Africa and Africa,
South America and African Americans,
Palestine, Palestine where was the world,
Where is the world with the UN, the hypocrite?

I don't understand why it happened, and happened,
And why it is happening and happening these days.
What I don't understand today and will not,
I wonder how they should understand it.
Beyond the pain and belittlement of the survivals,
Beyond the martyrdom and the death of the victims,
How should our grand, grand, grand-sons
And daughters understand it, understand it, how?
How should they actually believe it, believe it?

South Africa, South Africa,
Where was the world, where was the world
When in the mud in the dust you were thrown?
Where were the world and the UN, where,
Where, when you were suffering, bleeding, dying,
Where were they when your offspring's bloods
Were deep large rivers and were running faster,
Running, running faster along the rainy seasons,
Running, running faster along the dry seasons,
Running, running faster along the coldest seasons,
Running along the years along many decades?
Hypocrite, where were you . . . where were you?
The world hasn't been the world and is not,
And the UN remains the same leech.
Woï!

Africa, Africa,
Where was the world, where was the world
When the Slaves-masters were castrating
And spaying you to confine and
Keep you in the childhood of progress and freedom?
Ah, where was the world when you were suffering,
Weeping,
Bleeding,
Dying?
Where are the world and the UN, where,
Where are they as barbarities openly come back?
The world has not been the world,
The world is not yet the world,
And the UN has been and remains the same hypocrite,
The vampire-tooth of the vampire-imperialism;
Woï!

South America and African Americans,
Where were the world and the UN, where,
Where were they
When children became donkeys,
When adults became donkeys,
Patriarchs became donkeys,
Healthy people became donkeys,
And sick people became donkeys?
Where were they when children's bloods and sweat,
Adults' bloods and sweat and elders'
Were exquisite manures and gold that kneaded
And strengthened the vampire-capitalism?
And even today, where are they?

I am looking for the human face of the world
And I don't find it amid the scraps heap.
The world has not been the world and is not,
And the UN has been and remains the butchers' knife.
Woï!

Palestine, Palestine,
Where are the world and UN the gangster, where,
Where is the IPT, where; where are they,
As children's flesh and blood,
Youth's flesh and blood,
Adults' flesh and blood,
And elders' flesh and blood along the years
Constitute the bitumen and the crushed stones
Used to asphalt the highways of the great civilization?
The UN is not yet the UN,
The IPT is not yet the IPT;
When are they going to be fair to let the earth be free?
When is humanity going to slay the beast within?
Woï . . . when?

We watch all this,
We live all this,
We endure all this;
Pensively we go to bed everyday,
Pensively we wake up everyday
It is the blossom of our bosoms.
Our hearts have reached the climax of unhappiness,
Our hearts savour the ecstasy of pain,
But our minds our hearts are a cloudless lit moon,
Our minds our hearts are rid of clouds of revenge.

Colonization and slavery

They held slaves with strong ropes
And held them as if they were cows,
And hoped they could hold them for ever.
They captured and held our countries
As if they could never leave them.

And one day they said,
Never again, slavery is over!
And another day they said,
Never again, colonization is over!

But could slavery be over?
Could colonization be over?
It was simple that the enslaved
And the colonized looked at the roots
Of this filthy business and saw that
The way to freedom was far still.

Because they did not think of that,

Because they took for granted
what was said and swallowed,

Because there were no visible chains
gnawing at their feet and
savouring the blood,
Gnawing at their hands and
drinking the blood,

Because rains of lashes were not
Coming down on their bodies to wake up
Some red lavas of volcano,

Because the masters were not
sending the dogs any more to tear to pieces
those who disobeyed them,
and send a warning to the others,

Because the masters were not
Cutting some fingers, some hands,
Or arms or legs or killing openly any more
to punish the rebels,

Because people were not asked
To carry the masters' goods
From far distances to the train station
Or from inside of the continent to the coast,

Because the new form of slavery then
Consisted in paying them a salary
That would sweetly invite them and
Maintain them under the control of the masters,

Because the masters are the only ones
Who can tell them what is good or bad,
Tell them what is important or useless,
Tell them who is good and who is bad,

Because slaves and colonized never sat down,
Brushed and cleaned their minds
To remove the filthy mud and dust which
Were left there knowingly by the masters,

Slaves, colonized and their offspring
Until now are in the heavy chains still;
Heavy invisible burning chains,
Heavy invisible bloodthirsty chains,
Heavy invisible killing chains;
Nothing has changed, nothing has changed,
The situation worsens, worsens . . . worsens.

They lived and live in the submission still,
They lived and live in the terror still,
And the masters are strongly present than before;
Strongly present spiritually,
Strongly present physically,
Strongly present violently,
Culturally,
Economically,
Politically, politically . . . politically
In their lives, in their lives!
Nights, nights, what do you want?

Ah poor Africans and African descendants!
As I look at our wealthy continent,
I see human skeletons
Walk from place to place,
And in the West,
I see them wither daily,
Wither and wither like flowers
Harshly hit by a bad weather.

Washed in the sweats,
Washed in the pains,
Washed in the tears,
Washed in the bloods,
We are not desperate for our liberation.
For our liberation we are on our way.

Lions and cheetahs

Africans, is this the France you count on?
Africans, is this the England you count on?
Africans, is this the USA you count on?

See what they do! Hear what they say!
See what they do!
See what they do when it is sunny,
And what they do in the dark!
Hear what they say!
Hear what they say when sun is up,
And what they vomit out as the day
Lies down on the night's dark sheet!

Africans,
I want you to clearly understand that
These folks are but your worse foes.

As the herbivores stop sleeping deeply,
The carnivores experience tough times,
The relations between lions and cheetahs,
Or between jackals and hyenas
Strengthen and on the same territory,
Lions and cheetahs walk and hunt together,
Jackals and hyenas walk and hunt together.

Africans,
When is your while of relief in a year?
Africans, look at what you call friendship!
Are these the friends you count on?

Africans,
Until this day, the relations between you
And the West remain but what exists
Between the grazers and the big cats;
Do you realize? Don't doubt. Yes, it is.
Wake up, wake up; wake up, Africans!

Arms to the sky

Africans,
In the way they approach you,
In the way they deal with you,
In the way they treat you,
Do you see any kindness?
Do you see any kindness in them?
Do you see any divine steam spring
Out of them and come on you?

Take a deep breath,
Stop confusing yourselves
And calmly look at the way
They deal with you and treat you.
Look, look serenely at it!
And you lift your arms to the sky,
(Just as you were taught and fooled)
And repeatedly wail:

Help us, O God! Clean us!
Wash off our sins and put us up;
Get us out here,
Get us out of these sufferings,
Hear our tender words, O God!

Africans,
This is not the right way.
In the course of your life,
This is a catastrophic mistake.

The day I felt unsafe

The day I thought I was light
Like a dry leaf and weak,
I felt in love with the prayer house.

I was going there at least once a week
To worship, to look for peace;
I was going there at least once a week
To feel safe and protected;
But something happened,
Something unforgettable happened,
I saw something.
And on my mind it wonders still
Like a bad encounter a child has
That follows him all his life.

I saw something that day;
Something I was seeing daily in the city;
Something that was under my eyes
Threatening me in the markets,
restaurants,
work place,
parks,
my apartment:

a big criminal,
a strong monster,
the world's bloody executioner.

That day I felt unsafe in the prayer house,
I couldn't believe it; I quivered with fear.
I understood that the world was a rotten egg.

I left and decided I would never go back.
I stopped shaking.
I turned to myself and rapidly I explored
And turned myself to a protective land,
A land full of great caves;

As I discovered that the prayer house
Already was inside me,
I saw the uselessness of venturing elsewhere.
I saw no cloud neither fog of regret on my mind.

Wherever I could stand in life then (in a room,
Market, water, street, tree, work, nature . . .)
Suitably became but a prayer house.
I solved in a short while a problem
I for long thought was very tough:
I have sought and found safety in myself.

Many doors

Africa, what do you expect?
What do you expect from the West?
You hope the West will open you some doors.
Yes, the West will open you many doors;
May, many doors that open onto nothing;
With the West, you will see many doors open;
Many doors that always lead to nowhere;
Africa if you go with the West,
Be ready to love the leash,
Be ready to inhabit many caves,
Be ready for the everlasting slavery.

Africa, don't let me think

Africa, Africa
Don't let me think that you are empty,
or don't let me think that you are brave when
you are just a huge calabash full of holes.

Africa, Africa
If you are not cowardly or empty,
why can't I hear and see
Elephants create earthquake
hastening to the antelopes' rescue?
Africa, field of ambiguities, why?
Africa, field of absurdities, why?
Why can't I see and hear these Elephants?

Africa, Africa
I cannot hear serious defensive voices in the air;
I cannot hear some frightening roars in the sky
of the long nights of our humiliations;

Africa, Africa:
Africa, land of Samory Touré!
Africa, land of Chaka Zulu!
Where are you, Africa?
What have you become, Africa?

Africa, Africa:
Proud lion of yore,
shall you let all these conspiracies
Capture and swallow your children?

Africa, Africa
Why can't you say No
before foreigners come and say it?
Why can't you say Yes
before foreigners come and say it?
Or before they say No
where Yes is needed and
Yes where we need No?

Africa, Africa:
Proud gazelle of yore,
shall you fall
under the enemies' blows
without a leap?

Africans, God created us

Africans, God created us at his image,
We are the creatures by whom God exists.
In God or the gods we believe and trust
And in us they have put their trust.
Africans, we cannot let anybody humiliate us,
Africans, we cannot let any force terrorize us,
Africans, we cannot let any force weaken us,
Africans, we cannot let anybody wipe us out.

When we can let any of these things come to us,
It means that we refuse to honour ourselves,
And when we don't honour ourselves,
We are not honouring our Creator or our creators;
It means that we prefer submission and death,
It means that we voluntary choose to
Slay God,
Slay the gods.

Africans, we must live to keep the gods alive,
We must live to keep our ancestors alive
And to keep them omnipresent,
We must live to keep God alive.
Africans, it is imperious that we honour
The ones that honour us;
Africans, it is imperious that we come together
And fight for our survival.

Africans we know the path to total liberation,
But we weave tears to tie ourselves at inaction;
Africans we know the right way to liberation,
But we weave tears daily to strangle ourselves.
Strangling ourselves,
We strangle God.

Victims of democracy

Victims of the faceless western democracy,
Victims of the western fictive democracy,
Victims of the faceless western democracy
In Ivory Coast,
In Libya,
On many spots of Africa,
In the Third World;
Dear fallen ones:

Are you having a sweet sleep?
Or is it a bitter rest
Just at the taste of the life you lived?
Dear fallen ones:

Are you at ease?
Are you happy?
I wish you a long happiness and peace.
Dear fallen ones:

The forces of good are silenced;
Please support them,
Work with them;
Form the league of the dead
To help these forces defend our planet;
O dear fallen ones!

Many bleats

Many bleats from every corner come to my ears,
Pass my ears like hurried arrows on mission
And touch and launch a bloody revolution in my heart.
Peace and joy don't emanate from these bleats.
The bleats do not resound like those of the sheep and
Goats that live on good grasslands with good shepherds;
These bleats have no teeth and cannot wear a good smile.
I stop, I listen, I look. I see herds of sheep and goats.

On these sheep and goats dance countless fleas and lice.
They dance like a big colony of monkeys in the bush.
Where does this take place?—In Africa. On our land.
Who are the actors?—The leaders.
The people of Africa sucked and ruined by their leaders.

Africans, unless you get rid of this handful of parasites,
How can you be healthy, be gorgeous, grow and bloom?
Africans, the earthquakes have saddled on our heads.
We must throw them down and start a new life,
We must unmannerly throw them down.
African children, hear your mother's voice and stand up!
The enemies are very organized and very strong,
The enemies are well-equipped and powerful.
Brothers and sisters stand up! Let us come together!
Brothers and sisters let us patrol Africa together and
Like an army of ants, track and get rid of the enemies.

Mosquitoes, mosquitoes!

In the colonial days in Africa,
Before Africans became free on the paper,
Some white mosquitoes with short proboscises
And small abdomens used to suck Africans;
Mosquitoes, mosquitoes!

After the colonial days in Africa,
When Africans became free on the paper,
Some black mosquitoes with very long,
Very, very long proboscises and huge abdomens came;
These black mosquitoes were terrible,
These black mosquitoes are terrible.
Their long proboscises sink into the African wealth,
Their long proboscises sink into the Africans,
Pass the bones, reach the marrow and suck, suck . . .
Mosquitoes, mosquitoes!

When these black mosquitoes suck the Africans,
They rapidly fly and go
Deposit their loots in the western blood banks,
Come back and we hear their ever whining wings
Complain that their people are poor and need help;
And the bankers promise to help us
And we contact many debts, debts we never use.
Black mosquitoes, black mosquitoes!

Nowadays, African people are weighed down
By invisible white mosquitoes and visible black ones;
Nowadays, African people bend dangerously
Beneath the yoke of invisible white mosquitoes
And visible shameless black mosquitoes, ah!
Ah, bastards! Our land now teems with bastards.
The mosquitoes have put Africa naked like
Some wild cats that catch and eagerly
Pluck bushy guinea fowls alive and devour them.
Mosquitoes, mosquitoes, shameless mosquitoes!

And this day,
The malaria of poverty's stronger than ever.
And this day,
The yellow fever of agitations is stronger than ever.
Mosquitoes, mosquitoes, ah mosquitoes!

Heart, heart

Heart, heart,
Broken sad bleeding heart,
Let the rivers break out of your lakes.
Let them run; let them run and run . . .

They will wash you and wash;
They will turn you younger and stronger.

Heart, heart,
Broken sad bleeding heart,
You are not alone;
Let the rivers break out of your lakes.
You are not alone.
It is the law of life.
Even those happy hearts you see daily
Have their bleeding wounds;
Even these happy hearts you know
Have their bleeding wounds.
Even the happiest of hearts of the world
Have their bleeding wounds

Every smiling eye that we sight
Has a hidden drop of tear in the corner;
But we don't know; we don't see it.

Over there, there is one,
Here, there is one,
There, there is another one.
They are everywhere; everywhere.
You are not alone; it is pandemic.

Africans, Africans, look!

Africans, Africans, look!
The day is vandalized in Libya,
The day is tortured in Libya,
The day is suffocated in Libya,
The day is closing its eye in Libya,
The day is hastily deserting Libya.
The day is out of Libya; out.
Africans, can you imagine?
How can we ever return and
Stay in this dying sweet day?

Some Libyans don't know what
On their land is taking place,
And don't see what they are losing yet.
Some Africans who don't understand
The Western game don't know what
Africa is losing in Libya.
Africans, Africans, look!
Africans, what can we do?

Africans, how can this sweet day
Ever come back amid us?

People say that what is lost this season
Comes back the next season,
People say that nothing on earth is lost,
People say that what is lost will come back;
But what the Libyans have lost is lost.
What Africa has lost in Libya is lost.
It is lost. It will never come back,
It is lost, it is lost, lost, lost . . .
It is stolen, it is stolen; it is openly stolen.

The gangsters have openly robbed us,
They have openly robbed our big bank.
Libya, this unique African Eldorado
That has no debt will soon be in deep debt.
And if true patriots don't stand and say, No,
Many generations will pay the fictive debt.
Libyan patriots, African patriots:

Never give in about Libya. Fight, fight!

Some naïve and blind Libyans say that
They are patriots liberating their country;
They chase the rats away to let the bears,
Tigers, snakes and anacondas invade
And suffocate them all on their own land.
These bears, tigers, snakes and anacondas
Will blindly and harshly or softly kill;
Kill the youth,
Kill the children,
Kill the old,
Kill the born,
Kill the unborn for hundreds of years.
Ah, poor naïve liberators!
See what you have done to your country!

The good and the evil

The good was seated smiling at one side,
And the evil was seated laughing at its.
The good was in small number.
The evil was in great number.
In two unequal rows they were waiting.
One was almost twice the length of another.
They were waiting to be served.
The long row diminished, diminished
And finished so fast;
The evil was completely served.
The good was there waiting, waiting.
And before the dark,
The good was there seated, and waiting.

In the doomed days

In the doomed days,
In the doomed days
The poor will be helping the rich,
Will be helping the rich
To stand up and survive;

In the doomed days,
In the doomed days
The weak will be guiding the strong,
Will be guiding the strong;

In the doomed days,
In the doomed days
The most racist mouth
Will be whispering to the victims,
"Brothers, sisters, parents,
Friends, children, strangers,
I was wrong;
I love you so much, so much.
We are the same family,
We are the same, the same.
I was wrong;
I love you so much, so much.

In the doomed days,
In the doomed days
Glasses and dishes of Sufferings
Will be served to the arrogant,
Will be served to all the predators;
Will be served to all selfish hands;

In the doomed days,
In the doomed days
Those who steal and hide
Like mice and rats and squirrels
To ruin the economy of the families
And create poverty in the country
Will not stand the new life,
And will collapse one by one,
Collapse one by one; one by one
In the doomed days,
In the doomed days.

They say it

With a look and a smile full of smugness
And bursting with scorn, they talk
And talk and to finish they spout out:
—Servants, do you understand?

And answering as one,
Our leaders bow down lowly,
Bow down very lowly at the level
No leader ever went before,
And reverently say:
—Yes masters, yes masters.

—Servants do you understand?

And our people tenderly bow down,
Bow down very lowly:

—Yes great masters, yes yes yes yes . . .

We accept to be subhuman,
And not elsewhere
But on our own lands first,
And around the world;
We bend our sad faces,
We close our wet eyes
And pour out:
—Yes masters, yes, yes, yes yes . . .

They tell us that
If we need peace
We must fall asleep
And let them think,
Think for their people
And think for us.

Their acts
Tell us that
We are the children
As we were the children
And will remain the children.

Their acts
Ask us aloud
To obey them,
To sleep,
Sleep
And stand up,

With hunger
In our stomachs
Singing in unison
Like noisy termites
In an African bamboo,

And fall
On our knees
(All this must stop.)
And beg:

Daddy France,
Powerful France
(Though France knows
Very well how weak and poor she is.)
Please, please
Help us;

Daddy Uncle,
Please, please
Help us
Don't let us down
You can come and build
Many militaries camps
And do whatever you want,
But help us, help us;

Mammy England,
We didn't eat,
The children suffer from starvation,
The children are very weak.
Please, please
Help us;

Daddy Germany,
We never fought you,
Today's events
In the world
Tell us that
You were right
Hundred per cent,
Please, please
Help us;

New-born China,
Sit down like a king,
And show us the way
In our own countries,
Strong new-born
Please, please
Help us.

This must stop;
This African childish behavior must stop.

Broken-wings-pelican

Africa, broken-wings-pelican!
Africa, for long you were tortured
And altered by unknown diseases;

Africa, the recent years and this day
Have led us to know all about you,
We, your sons and daughters from
The north to the south, and east to west;

Africa, for long we doubted and waited,
Until recently, we saw clearly the faces
Of the beasts hidden in your flesh;

Knowing now what you suffer from,
Africa you will heal and grow faster.

Africa, broken-wings-pelican,
Your offsprings and time
Will quickly fix your wings;

And Africa, you will leave the shore,
You will return on the air,
And reconnect with the high sea,
And bravely fight for your dignity.

Africa, this is Africa I dream of.

If I were an African politician

If I were an African politician,
I would be known for these words
and be seen putting them in action:

'I know what the tomatoes flowers
lead me to. I know.
I know, I know, I know.
but I don't see where
the roses can take me to. Where?
maybe to the sky or under the ground!
But not to my needy people;
My needy people are not in the sky,
they are not under the ground,
and I don't want to see them
under it either in the sky;
I know that they are here,
I know they love to be here,
and they must see me.
I know what the tomatoes flowers
lead me to. I know, I know.'

If I were an African politician,
I would be known for these words.

Our lands

Our lands are gorgeous rich trees
On which the birds of prey have settled,
Feel free,
Feel happy,
And do not dream to ever abandon them.
These birds' interests are a ceaseless lightning
That greets the trees and goes,
Greets the trees and goes.

They vandalize and deprave the trees,
They organize the fights on each of the boughs,
Tear out the trees' leaves, and drain the trees' sap.
What can stop these fights on our trees?
How can peace be on our trees?
How can they bear flowers and yield good fruits?
When can pigeons build stable nests on and blossom?
How can birds' songs warm our trees?

Our lands' wealth arrogantly smiles at the world.
Our lands are great trees run by the birds of prey.
Ah long African night!

We wait patiently

Life on our land becomes untenable.
The preachers ask us to await the miracles.
We wait patiently and hopefully.

Life on our land becomes unbearable.
The authorities talk of bright future.
We wait patiently and hopefully.

Life's conditions deteriorate,
Things decay, rust, collapse.
We hope, we hope and wait.
We wait, we wait, wait and get nothing.

Alas, we understand at last
That nothing will come.
Our preachers do lie,
Our authorities do lie.

We wait patiently and hopefully.
We wait for the light
To appear in our sky and
Swoop down on the night we are in.
This is to be very irresponsible
This is the childish approach.
If we want to grow,
If we choose to be free,
If we choose to leave the night,
We must noisily
Drop down
Our childish thoughts;

People,
Look, look!
That light is already in us;
That light is always in us.
But saddled with the night,
We wait for the light to come.

People,
Drop it down,
Drop it down,
Drop the childish seed of your mind,
And,
Take off.

We understand that we must not wait.
We are the source of light,
We are the source of miracles,
We are the source of our bright future.
We are the light the miracles the bright future.
Our preachers do lie.
Our authorities do lie.

Foreigners, visit Africa

Some people think that Africa is a joyless place.
From afar, some think that Africa equals sadness.
It is true that many things happen to Africa,
Come by man's hand or naturally and hurt Africa
And make it look like the saddest of place lands.

But we Africans are a special people on earth.
We keep our balance amid hellish tragedies;
Tragedies which elsewhere could seriously flatten
Or wipe off the people at the continental scale,
Or make them look like a new species of animals;
We Africans are a special people on earth,
And mostly the Blacks scattered over the world;

But we don't give in despite all these blows.
We don't at all; our tailless Africa is full of joys.
Foreigners, stop knowing our Africa through hearsays.
Foreigners, visit Africa to discover our true Africa.

Move closer to our African brothers and sisters
And you will learn a lot of helpful things.
You'll learn the art of living in peace within the chaos.
You will learn to be ready for the doomed days.

You will learn that people are not happy in Africa
Because their efforts are crowned with successes;
You will amazingly discover that they are not joyous
Because they have a lot of clothes to wear
Or enough food and drink to take everyday;

They know that the amount of gold
That one possess does not always bring joy;
They know that happiness and joy are not necessary
In a good health or the size of the daily meal;
Their joy and happiness come from many sources.

On the face of a Westerner that has a whole cow meat,
I don't perceive the great joy and happiness
Of the Africans who gather to share a guinea fowl;
On the face of a Westerner whose freezer
And fridge are full of foods and whose closets
Have every kind of clothes and shoes,
I don't find the peace, the joy and the happiness
Which woo and stay on the face
Of an African peasant or a city dweller
That possesses only:

Two pairs of shoes,
Four clothes,
One woody toothbrush,
No freezer,
No fridge,
With the morning meal grasped from the farm,
With the evening meal grasped from the farm,
With a daily food intake very poor
That is bought on the street,
No bank card,
No bank account,
No credit card,

No bills,
No debts,
No stress . . .

Foreigners, visit Africa to learn about it,
To amazingly witness people's laughter and smiles
Jump highly and stab the deep night in the face;
Visit Africa to learn that it's not always the night
All the time, everywhere in Africa;
Visit Africa to learn about the peace, the joy,
And the happiness of my tailless Africa;
Foreigners, stop knowing our Africa through hearsays.
Visit Africa, foreigners; visit our Africa.

Like the ancient Egypt

Just like the ancient great Egypt went down
And slept under the rule of a dark-skin Pharaoh,
A potent shining modern nation slowly shakes,
Quietly bends and noisily kisses the night
Under a leader who is of the same skin.

We vote them

We vote them and they promise
To come back the next day
And work with us for us.
We vote them.

When they go,
We seldom see them again.
When they go,
They spend time mastering
The art of being subtle;

And the few whiles they come,
It is to spatter our minds
With their bikes of scorn;

And the few whiles they come,
It is to spatter our hearts
With their bikes of arrogance;

And the few whiles they come,
It is to provoke our tears
With their bikes of treasons,

Or to ask us to come out
And vote them again.
Divided as we remain,
Some hands always go ahead
And keep them there.

Song of tomorrow

Tomorrow when we take the stick
And get out of the night as David leaving Egypt,
We will live a happy life,
We will look back as we move forward.
And chant regretfully but proudly:

We didn't make any progress.
For a very long time we stayed in the cyst.
We thought that some hands
Were going to push us,
We thought that some hands
Were going to liberate us,
But since we realized we were wrong,
See how far we have advanced!
Since we convinced ourselves
That we could do it,
See how far we have advanced!

We made only one mistake,
And it cost us some big losses;
We drew and tied ourselves
On the giant rocks of status quo with
The ropes of apathy and discrimination;
At last we are awake.

The foreign tools

If we don't grasp and hold the foreign tools
With our moral perfumes and keep them here,
We will get lost like the developed countries;
We will stab ourselves in the chest.

A message to the world

Africans,
Facing the cruelties and the bloodshed
Of the oppressors on our own land,
We have stopped resisting openly,
We have stopped fighting openly
And they think that they have subjected us.
We haven't given in even for one second,
And will never sleep before the oppressors.

Oppressors, don't dance, don't rejoice!
Any water that leaves its bed is not dead,
Any water that deserts its bed is always somewhere,
In the air, in a plant or under the ground;

Facing the cruelties and the bloodshed,
Our resistance has tactically left,
Our fight has tactically left;
They have abandoned our hands,
Abandoned our lips,
Abandoned our pens,
Abandoned our eyes
And found refuge to our marrows.

Our resistance and fight are active volcanoes,
And the oppressors cannot see them;
Our resistance and our fight grow very fast;
They grow stronger and stronger from the marrows.
The oppressors think that the volcanoes are dead,
And around them and even inside their mouths
They build luxurious houses, farm the land,
Extract the mines stir the waters and the air,
Tame the sun and the wind;
But we will never sleep before the oppressors.

Africans,
Send a great message to the world.
Africans,
Tell those who always rape Africa
That you are entering a new era.

Africans,
Tell all the foreigners and
All your ungrateful sons and daughters
Who want to rape Africa
economically,
culturally,
financially,
psychologically,
and morally
that everything will shift,
that in this process the rapists
will be henceforth raped;

Africans,
Tell these criminals that
Your new strong sex
Will leave on them deadly wounds
That neither a surgeon
Nor a psychologist can ever sew.
Africans,
Send this warning message to them;
Send it to those who around the world
Love to prey on us and go or stay.